From God's Hands
To Your Land

— *Blessings!*

Table of Contents

1 extra copy of the Title Deed is on page 72

From one man he made all the nations, that
they should inhabit the whole earth;
and he marked out their appointed times
in history and the boundaries
of their lands.   —Acts 17:26 (NIV)

If my people, which are called by my name,
shall humble themselves, and pray, and seek my face,
and turn from their wicked ways; then will I hear from
heaven, and will forgive their sin,
and will heal their land. —2 Chronicles 7:14

Introduction

The Bible establishes the spiritual relationship between God and His land. The Lord desires to pour out His blessings on your land, but scripture says that His blessings can be blocked. The Word reveals how previous events that took place on the land by us, our ancestors, former owners, or past inhabitants of the land, can cast a cloud on the title of the land.

Land has a testimony, which is its heritage. Many communities have erected memorials to commemorate what happened years ago on some historical property site. Like the buildings that you can see on top of it, there are hidden structures in place underneath. What is beneath can be causing problems for what, or who, is above. When you inherit, purchase or rent property, it's spiritual heritage comes with along with it. Scriptures that prove this are found within this book.

The Lord, as the Owner of the original title deed of all real estate, gave us the responsibility to subdue and take dominion over the land we are appointed to, whether you are a renter or an owner of the land. (Acts 17:26) The Lord has called each of us to be ambassadors of reconciliation on behalf of our land. (2 Chronicles 7:14)

Included are step-by-step instructions, with prayers and decrees to recite as you reconcile and redeem your land, which will ensure that His blessings will flow freely on your land with no hindrances. Included is a symbolic spiritual Title Deed that will serve as a written declaration that your property has been redeemed and is free and clear of any spiritual demonic liens or curses. The practical applications of the information contained in this book will form a powerful combination that will inspire you to action and will enable you to set your land free of any curses. The reconciliation ceremony takes about 15 minutes.

Don't live another day under a cloud of guilt that may be encompassing you and your property. Call on the Name that is above all names to save us from any sin, and live in the freedom and prosperity that He promised us.

*The Lord considers us to be the trustees
of <u>His</u> land. The land we live on has been
entrusted to us by the Lord for safekeeping, care,
and management. We are groundskeepers.*

Chapter 1
The Title Deed

As Creator of the Earth, the Lord is the Holder of the Title Deed

When the Lord created the earth, He became the first owner of what became the starting point of the real estate called the earth. The Lord makes it clear that He is the title deed owner of the land, and that we are only temporary residents of it, working with Him to develop it.

> *The land shall not be sold into perpetual ownership, for the land is mine; you are only strangers and temporary residents with me.* --Leviticus 25:23 (AMP)

On the 6th day of creation, the Lord created man from the dust of the earth and established a divine connection, a bond between man and the land.

> *And the Lord God formed man of the dust of the ground, and breathed into his nostrils the breath of life; and man became a living soul.* –Genesis 2:7

God assigned the responsibility for the land to man

> *And the Lord God took the man, and put him into the Garden of Eden to tend, guard, and keep it.* --Genesis 2:15 (AMP)

To *tend* means to develop. We are to be developers of the land the Lord has assigned to us, for His purposes.

We are assigned land as a portion of our inheritance in the Will and Testament of the Lord. He has willed it to us temporarily while we are on the earth, and set up for us in a trust. The Lord considers us to be the trustees of <u>His</u> land. The land we live on has been entrusted to us by the Lord for safekeeping, care, and management. We are His grounds-keepers. The word *trustee* means; a person appointed to hold

1

property, to take care of, and apply the same for the benefit of those entitled to it.

The Lord has a specific plan for our land. He defined the borders of the geographical location of the land where we are to live before we were born. The location where you live right now is your God assigned boundary of habitation.

And hath made of one blood all nations of men for to dwell on all the face of the earth, and hath determined the times before appointed, and the bounds of their habitation. -- Acts 17:26

We might think of the place we occupy simply as a physical address, not our God-chosen destination, but this destination has a God-given responsibility attached to it. Each individual who has given their life to the Lord is responsible to tend, guard, and keep their specific geographical location of land where the Lord has placed them. This would mean spiritually, through prayer, and physically, through proper land management for the most fruitfulness. If we do not do this we have violated the trust the Lord has placed in us.

You might be thinking, I don't want to tend this soil. I want to move from it. The Lord may be willing for you to move, but has an assignment for you to complete with the land before you leave it.

It is your promised land whether it seems like it or not. You are to take dominion over it for a season of your life, however long the Lord may have you there. Possibly, after you settle things for the land in the spiritual realm by reconciling it to the Lord, you might be released to leave and go on to a land assignment in another area, or you might lose your desire to leave.

The Garden of Eden
The sin of disobedience that Adam and Eve committed against God caused them to be driven out of the beautiful garden. Their disobedience forced God, as the Righteous Judge of heaven and earth, to pronounce a judgment against the land, with repercussions to come upon them and the land for their sin.

Unto the woman He said: I will greatly multiply your sorrow, and your conception; in pain you shall bring forth children; your desire shall be for your husband, and he shall rule over you. Unto Adam he said, because thou hath hearkened unto the voice of thy wife, and hast eaten of the tree of which I commanded thee, saying, Thou shalt not eat of it; cursed is

2

the ground for thy sake; in sorrow shalt thou eat of it all the days of thy life.   ---Genesis 3:16-17

This same judgment executed by the Judge of heaven and earth centuries ago is still visibly in effect today.   Just as we accept the blessings promised to God's people as they flow down through the generations, we have to understand the curses flow down also, until they are legally stopped in the spiritual realm.

The birth pains that a woman goes through to birth a baby is evidence of the curse put upon Eve. A friend of mine said she read that scripture as she was approaching the birth of her second child. She decided to stand in the gap for the sin Eve committed against the Lord, repenting and asking for forgiveness. She asked the Lord to lift the sentence of birth pains off of her. She has had contractions without pain for the last two of her three children.

In order to bring forth the fruit of the land, man is constantly trying to stay ahead of the insect population and various disasters of nature that continue to occur. These examples are a few of many in scripture that reveal the spiritual ramifications due to sin committed upon the land, and how it transfers into the physical realm and those living on it.

The enemy uses sin as his legal right to gain access to our land. Sin gives him permission to execute a judgment or lien, which is a debt against the land that can only be paid and redeemed through the blood of Jesus. Another word that could be used in place of *lien,* in the spiritual realm, is *curse*.

Our God is a Righteous Judge who is required by His Word to honor the legal rights of these liens. A spiritual legal claim like this against a piece of property can restrict the use of the property. If the lien isn't paid in full in the spiritual realm, as the land is sold in the physical many times, spiritual liens and their consequences can be passed along. As different owners take possession of a piece of property, and each new owner sins upon the land, it adds another lien.

In the physical realm, if a lien is placed against a property it is legally attached to the property as a debt or liability. In many instances the lien holder has to give approval for changes to be made. In order to make alterations to the property for improvement, sometimes that debt has to be paid in full.

Just as the old unrenewed man in us can hold us back in our spiritual walk, old things that are present on our land can prevent the new thing the Lord wants to perform in our geographical location from happening. In the natural realm, soil has to be prepared to be fruitful. Fallow ground has to be broken up. Old dead things that might be in the soil must not just be cut off, but uprooted and cast out. One of those things, which seems as though it were dead but is very much alive, might be blood that may have been shed on the land.

Blood that has been shed upon land cries out

We see the example of how blood shed on our land has a voice in the spiritual realm that is heard loud and clear in the Courtroom of Heaven.

> *And Cain talked with Abel his brother, and it came to pass, when they were in the field, that Cain rose up against Abel his brother, and slew him. And the Lord said unto Cain, Where is thy brother? And he said," I know not: Am I my brother's keeper? And he said, what hast thou done, the voice of thy brother's blood crieth unto me from the ground. And now thou are cursed from the earth, which hath opened her mouth to receive thy brother's blood from thy hand. When thou tillest the ground, it shall not henceforth yield unto thee her strength; a fugitive and a wanderer shalt thou be in the earth.*
> *-- Genesis 4:8-12*

Inheriting or purchasing land with a blood curse on it

We see from the story of Cain and Abel that if there has been bloodshed on the land, the blood has a voice. The sin needs to be atoned for so the land can enter into a rest. The blood on the land cries out for justice. Cain was personally cursed by God to be a wanderer, never at peace, and whatever land he lived on was also cursed. The Lord is specific about how he will deal with the sin of bloodshed.

> *For behold, the LORD comes out of His place To punish the inhabitants of the earth for their iniquity; The earth will also disclose her blood, And will no more cover her slain. – Isaiah 26: 21 (NKJV)*

Another example of this curse due to innocent blood being shed on land is found in Deuteronomy 19:10.

> *Lest innocent blood be shed in your land, which the Lord Your God gives you as an inheritance, and so blood guilt be upon you.*

In the Old Testament, God made provision to redeem the land from the curse of innocent blood shed upon it, through the use of the blood of sacrificed animals. The Lord required blood for blood.

If someone is found slain...Then all the elders of the town nearest the body shall wash their hands over the heifer whose neck was broken in the valley, and they shall declare: "Our hands did not shed this blood, nor did our eyes see it done. Accept this atonement for your people Israel, whom you have redeemed, LORD, and do not hold your people guilty of the blood of an innocent person." Then the bloodshed will be atoned for, and you will have purged from yourselves the guilt of shedding innocent blood, since you have done what is right in the eyes of the LORD. —Deuteronomy 21:1,6-9 (NIV)

You shall not thus pollute the land in which you live; for blood pollutes the land, and no expiation can be made for the land, for the blood that is shed in it, except by the blood of him who shed it. —Numbers 35: 33 (RSV)   (Expiation: to atone)

...and almost all things are by the law purged with blood and without shedding of blood is no remission. —Hebrews 9:22

The responsible party for the bloodshed may not be available, so he or she can't make restitution. But we, as intercessors, those called by the Lord to stand in the gap and make up the hedge, can petition the Lord, repenting on behalf of sin committed against the Lord by the shedding of blood on the land, and ask His forgiveness. Jesus spoke to the multitudes in the New Testament about this curse of bloodshed coming upon the people. He leveled a charge against them for blood shed on the ground.

Wherefore, behold I send unto you prophets, and wise men, and scribes: and some of them ye shall kill and crucify; and some of them shall ye scourge in your synagogues, and persecute them from city to city; That upon you may come all the righteous blood shed upon the earth, from the blood of the righteous Abel unto the blood of Zacharias son of Barachias as, whom ye slew between the temple and the altar.
—Matthew 23:34-35

It is clear that if there has been bloodshed on the land you are living on, it has to be atoned for. If not, you will reap the consequences even though you might not have had any knowledge of it.

If you have any doubts that blood still speaks, then look to the example of the shed blood of Jesus for our sins. It still speaks. Don't live another day under a cloud of guilt that may be encompassing your property and you. Call on the Name that is above all names to save us from any sin, and live in the freedom and prosperity that He promised us.

5

*In himself, man does not have
the authority to clear spiritual liens
against the title of the property.*

Chapter 2
Signs Of A Curse

Signs of a curse on land that affects the people living on it
Breaking God's laws and the worship of foreign gods (idols) on the land
are guaranteed to open a door for a curse to gain legal access.

> *And first I will recompense their iniquity and their sin double;*
> *because they have defiled my land, they have filled mine*
> *inheritance with the carcasses of their detestable and*
> *abominable things. –Jeremiah 16: 18*

A curse can come onto a piece of land if someone buries something on
the property to bring good luck.

Luck: A force that brings good fortune or adversity.

Force: active power. This force of luck is active, but not of God.

> *As the bird by wandering, as the swallow by flying, so the*
> *curse causeless shall not come. -- Proverbs: 26:2*

According to the Word, a curse can't come without a valid reason. A
violation of God's Word would give a curse a valid reason to come.

There is a hidden root somewhere for everything we see. That is not to
say that every trial is due to a curse, but it is important to close the
door that could be allowing the curse that is causing the problem. If
problems persist, then look for another cause somewhere else.

The following is another example of a curse leveled against the land and
how it affected the people because of sin. In Egypt, Pharaoh wouldn't let
the Hebrews celebrate a feast to their God.

> *And afterward Moses and Aaron went in, and told Pharaoh,*
> *Thus saith the LORD God of Israel, Let my people go, that they*

7

may hold a feast unto me in the wilderness. —Exodus 5:1

Because Pharaoh, the ruler of the land, wouldn't allow the Jewish people to worship their God, a curse came upon the Pharaoh and the physical land of Egypt in the form of plagues.

An important thing to note is that the Israelites, who were living in the midst of Egypt in an area called Goshen, were not affected by the plagues. The Lord says He did this as a testimony to the Egyptians that He was capable of protecting His own people even in the midst of all of the plagues.

> *But on that day I will deal differently with the land of Goshen, where my people live; no swarms of flies will be there, so that you will know that I, the Lord, am in this land. I will make a distinction between my people and your people. This miraculous sign will occur tomorrow. --Exodus 8:22-23 (NIV)*

Other references to this setting apart of God's people and their land are found in Exodus 9:5-7,26.

We can live in a Goshen in the midst of an Egypt. God is looking for opportunities for us to become living testimonies before our neighbors and others in our communities. We will be witnesses of His goodness and provision that He extends to those who belong to Him. As we re-covenant our land and homes to Him, He will do this.

Back to the story....

> *And the LORD said unto Moses, Say unto Aaron, Stretch out thy rod, and smite the dust of the land, that it may become lice throughout all the land of Egypt. --Exodus 8:16*

Because of an experience we had when we went on a mission trip to Ghana, West Africa several years ago, I believe that the Pharaoh curse is still in operation. The story of the trip is recorded in the next few pages.

In 2006, my husband, Bud, and I were members of a team that traveled to Ghana, West Africa on a mission trip. The Lord told us He was going to perform great signs and wonders in "Egypt/Africa", as He called it, while we were there. We later learned that in ancient days Lower Egypt included what is now called Africa.

The Lord said that he wanted to use Egypt/Africa as a place of refuge once again. As we were praying with friends about the upcoming trip, they said they felt the Lord told them that they were to come with us, but first they were to go to Israel and get water out of the Jordan River and bring it with them to Africa, which they did.

During the final planning stages of the trip, we realized that the dates were the exact time of the Passover centuries ago, when the Jews were leaving Egypt after being set free from the bondage of slavery under the rule of the Egyptians and their foreign gods.

We wanted to celebrate the Passover while in Egypt/Africa, so we gathered the physical items we would need to share the Passover meal with the host church leadership. We celebrated the Passover meal and teaching with the church elders and pastor. The atmosphere was very spiritually charged with the Holy Spirit as we considered the fact that the Lord had brought us to this very land at the exact time that the Passover had occurred thousands of years ago and, at the same time, was being celebrated by Jews and Christian alike all over the world.

We planned a medical crusade during the daytime. We were told that the Muslim people who lived in the area would come to get medicine. We were hoping to reach these people with the gospel as they came for the medicine.

For three of the days of the trip, a medical tent was set up on the school grounds in a predominantly Muslim neighborhood. In the evenings we were set up for a Praise and Worship Crusade on these same grounds, which was a miracle in itself. Large speakers broadcast the services, and those in the surrounding neighborhoods could hear plainly. We taught about worship and praise to God, and how that would defeat our enemies.

With us were an optometrist (eye doctor) and 2 young graduate nurses who worked in the baby ward of the hospital. Every day we would treat many people. They would stand in long lines, some sitting in white plastic lawn chairs, waiting for us when we got there in the morning.

After the triage, each person was given a slip with their vitals and their complaints. They would then move to one of the many groups of three people, usually one pastor from a church in the city and two intercessors, with at least one from our team. Each group would pray with and for the patient. They would ask the person if they believed in Jesus, and would pray for them however the conversation led. Some deliverances occurred, which created a bit of noise at times, but was a testimony to those waiting.

After prayer, the card with their medical condition would be handed to me to read. My job at home was in a Family Medical Clinic. One facet of my job at home was to hand out medicine prescribed to the patient and give instruction as to how to take it, so I volunteered for that part in the crusade. I would read each card and hand out the medicine and directions to the nurses, who would then pass it on to the people. We were all very surprised to note that no one had complained of headaches, neck or back pain. All week we had been seeing the women carrying heavy loads on top of their heads, everything from large bowls of fruit, to heavy sewing machines. We saw one man walking down the street with a load of wooden chairs on top of his head.

I mention this because the Lord wanted the people to recognize me as one who knew their medical complaints. I was to be the speaker on the last night of the crusade and I was seeking the Lord all week for His message for these people, to bring them hope. On the night before I was to speak, I woke up at 4:00 a.m. I knew the Lord wanted to reveal something to me so I got up and quietly slipped into the bathroom. I felt led of the Holy Spirit to look up the story of the Passover in Exodus.

I turned to the story in Exodus Chapters 6 through 12. The Lord told Moses to ask Pharaoh to let the Hebrew children go out to the desert to worship their God. Pharaoh denied the request, so the Lord began to use Aaron and Moses as His human ambassadors to decree curses to come upon Egypt/Africa. As I read through the curses, I became aware that the complaints of the people we had been treating all week in the medical crusade were symptoms of the curses leveled against Pharaoh and the land of Egypt/Africa. It became apparent the curse against the land was still in effect and plaguing the people.

God's dealings with Egypt are commonly called plagues because of the main Hebrew verbs that describe God's actions: I will strike (Exodus 7:17) and I will smite (Exodus 8:2). This reinforces God's judgment behind them. Many of the plagues are aimed at Egypt's nature gods as much as at the Egyptians themselves. God demonstrated that the various Egyptian gods are powerless and judged by Him. (Numbers 33:4) Below is a list of the curses and how they are affecting the people of Egypt/ Africa today.

The Blood Curse: A curse against the god of the Nile, all waters of Egypt---in streams, rivers, ponds, pools, and all vessels in the homes. The river Nile was worshipped by the Egyptians under various names and symbols. It was called the father of life, and the father of the gods; thus the first miracle was a blow to the gods of Egypt.

The Egyptians abhorred blood, and their horror must have been extreme when they saw their sacred river and all other water in their country turned to blood. To this day, most of the water sources throughout Egypt/Africa are not safe to drink. People get all kinds of diseases related to drinking the bad water, with parasites and fevers being a major problem. The people had complained of fevers and parasites.

The Frog Curse: The goddess of childbirth, creation and grain germination was depicted as a frog, or a woman with the head of a frog, betraying her connection with water. As a water goddess, she was also a goddess of fertility. We had lots of complaints of infertility and difficulty getting pregnant.

The Lice Curse: Lice are a parasite to animals and man. The lice came out of the dust. This curse was against the dust and the insect god. This could have been ticks, lice, gnats, or mosquitoes, all of which existed in the dry, hot climate of Egypt. Mosquitoes carry diseases, and we know how many people suffer with malaria in Africa because of mosquitoes. Visitors have to take preventative medicine, which aren't always effective. A complaint of the people was complications from malaria.

The Flies Curse: This plague was designed to manifest the helplessness of the god of the flies, who was supposed to have power to prevent flies. The magicians couldn't stop the flies. This was a severe blow to idolatrous worship in Egypt.

The Boils Curse: This curse was against the goddess of medicine and peace. The Lord told Aaron and Moses to take handfuls of ashes from a furnace and throw them up into the air. He said it would become fine dust in all the land of Egypt and it would cause boils to break out as sores upon man and beast. The furnace the dust came from was a smelting furnace for metals. The word used refers to the smoke of Sodom, so the word is not limited to a smelting furnace. Here it could mean the place of human sacrifice where such offerings were made in the fire to appease the gods. A chief complaint from the people was boils and burning and itching eyes. They said it was as though there was sand in their eyes that wouldn't come out.

11

<u>The Hail Curse:</u> The plague that destroyed livestock could have been an attack on the goddess of the sky. Weather problems of too much rain, then too little, have played havoc on the food supply.

<u>The Locust Curse:</u> God of storms and disorder. Food shortages are a constant problem all over Africa/Egypt.

<u>The Plague of Darkness:</u> The darkening of the sun had a two-fold effect. First, God demonstrated His power over the sun, the most potent religious symbol of Egypt. Second, it was a direct frontal attack on Pharaoh himself, since he was considered to be the incarnation of the sun god. To this day, Africa is called the "Dark Continent." The Lord wants to turn it into a continent of light.

<u>Death of the First-Born:</u> Pharaoh was considered the ultimate power of Egypt. But he had felt enough of the effects of being cursed by the powerful God of the Hebrews, up to and including the death of his first-born son that he finally let them go.

> *And it came to pass, that at midnight the LORD smote all the firstborn in the land of Egypt, from the firstborn of Pharaoh that sat on his throne unto the firstborn of the captive that was in the dungeon; and all the firstborn of cattle.*
> *—Exodus 12:29*

As I read the account, I was amazed and excited to think about what the Lord had in mind for the people. That evening I explained to the people about the Jewish Passover Feast and exodus out of Egypt. I read to them the curses and the symptoms that came with each curse. As the people recognized they were suffering under the same curses, they began to cry out in repentance to God. It was an amazing time. Many were supernaturally healed and delivered, both physically and spiritually.

We held a repentance ceremony. Bud, who has Jewish blood in his linage, prayed publicly before the people with our African pastor. The pastor stood in the gap for the Egyptian/African ruler that caused these curses to come upon the people, repenting before the Lord, and asking forgiveness.

Bud stood in the gap for the Jewish people, to receive forgiveness on their behalf. Daniel did this for the Israelites (see Daniel 9:1-10). We led the people in a prayer of repentance and forgiveness. We asked that the Lord cleanse them, us, and the land from all curses, that He remove the principalities that had ruled the land, due to the legal right they had, and to set everyone and their land free and heal them of all the side effects of the curses.

Bud and the pastor took communion together, as a visible symbol of redemption and renewing of the covenant with the Lord God of the heavens and the earth.

The team member that had gone to Israel to get water from the Jordan River poured it on the land, as another symbol of cleansing and healing, giving the land a new spiritual baptism. Afterward, a pastor from the area came up and told us that one of the main principalities they dealt with in that geographical location was named Marine, the water god.

We returned to the area two years later and we saw oil rigs all along the coast. When we asked about them, we were told that the United States was drilling for oil and, if they found it, Ghana would receive large financial revenues. A few months later I picked up a newspaper that included an article that said Ghana would receive 3 billion dollars in oil revenue in 2009, due to the discovery of oil along the coast of Ghana. (Oil is a symbol of light.)

> *In that day there will be an altar to the Lord in the heart of Egypt, and a monument to the Lord at its border. It will be a sign and a witness to the Lord almighty in the land of Egypt.*
> *—Isaiah 19: 19-20a (NIV)*

I am sure we will continue to see physical and spiritual results (revival) because of the curses being broken. I am not saying that millions of prayers on behalf of Africa over the centuries aren't valuable. We each have our part, and working together we can take back the land. In His timing, the Lord supernaturally is bringing His illumination and brightness to Egypt/Africa.

The Lord plans that we act as advocates for our land

The Lord has a plan for each of us that will defeat our enemies and remove the hold they have on our land. His plan is for us to each be an "Ambassador of Reconciliation".

> *Their Redeemer is strong; the LORD of hosts is his name: he shall thoroughly plead their cause, that he may give rest to the land, and disquiet the inhabitants of Babylon.—Jeremiah 50:34*

We intercede through repentance to bring about reconciliation. As intercessors, we stand in the gap on behalf of sin committed upon a piece of land. We ask forgiveness, petitioning the Lord to cleanse the land of all iniquity, to set it free, reconciling it to Himself, and clear the title of all liens or curses.

> *If my people, which are called by my name, shall humble themselves, and pray, and seek my face, and turn from their wicked ways; then will I hear from heaven, and will forgive their sin, and will heal their land.* —2 Chronicles 7: 14 (NIV)

The Lord wants the property that we live on to be as beautiful and prosperous as the Garden of Eden was when He created it for Adam and Eve.

> *And all things are of God, who hath reconciled us to himself by Jesus Christ, and hath given to us the ministry of reconciliation; To wit, that God was in Christ, reconciling the world unto himself, not imputing their trespasses unto them; and hath committed unto us the word of reconciliation.* —2 Corinthians. 5:18-19

The definition of the word *reconciliation:* To cover over, atone for sin; make atonement for sin and persons by legal rites. (#3722 Strong's Concordance)

In himself, man does not have the authority to clear spiritual liens against the title of the property

Only the Lord, who is the Righteous Judge of heaven and earth, in whose Courtroom the enemy has been presenting the case against our land, has the authority to forgive the sin and remove the legal rights of the enemy to our land. After legal protocol has been followed, the Judge will give the motion to order the removal of liens from the title.

The Lord Jesus Christ is the only one who has the authority to forgive sin, but He has given us, his blood bought redeemed people, legal power of attorney on the earth to act on his behalf.

> *But that ye may know that the Son of man hath power on earth to forgive sins.* —Mark 2:10

The Lord extends His mercy in justice. As we walk with Him, obedient to His principals, He is able to extend mercy and forgiveness.

If we accept Him into our lives then are disobedient to His Word, the Righteous Judge is forced to judge us. If we insist on walking in sin a door is opened to the enemy.

14

Patterns reveal the possibility of a curse in action

If we notice unfavorable patterns (which have been called "bad luck") for the people living on the property, we should take action through prayer before we purchase the property. Don't be afraid to ask questions about previous owners because the source or root of the problem can be hidden, and a person might not realize these problems are symptoms of a curse. People can exhaust every avenue in the natural they can think of, and not be able to stop the problems. They may never realize that the source of the hardship they are under is from a curse that came with the land they purchased.

They may begin to think that the Lord is punishing them for some unknown reason. The enemy will attack them with unbelief and doubt. This could explain why a person could lose a piece of property, through no fault of their own, with circumstances that could be explained in the natural as an excuse for what is happening. This could effectively hide the real cause. The true root problem might never be exposed and dealt with. Everything visible has been birthed from something that was once invisible.

A man shared with me a testimony about buying a repossessed home. He and his wife had been doing well financially up to that point. Within a few months of purchasing the home he lost his job unexpectedly. It looked like they might lose the house. He took the information in this book and prayed over the property, removing the curses, clearing the spiritual title, dedicating the property to the Lord. Within a couple of weeks he was hired by a company that offered him a great job with better pay than his last job, and they were soon back on track. They didn't lose the house.

In the physical realm, the laws that govern the transfer of property from one buyer to another require a title search to protect the person buying the property. We should take care of the business of the spiritual title search before we purchase property, as much as it is possible. The possibility of a curse shouldn't stop us, but we need to be armed with knowledge so we could ward off possible financial disaster.

A Christian could be an innocent victim who rents or purchases a piece of property that has a curse attached to it. They could begin to reap the fruit of the curse within their family. They might suffer from financial, physical or mental health problems. Any of these could indicate the presence of a curse.

Here is yet another testimony about the affect of curses, from Kip and Keri.

My wife and I noticed what we would call negative spiritual activity in our home that began shortly after we moved in. There were areas in our home that we would describe as dark and cold. This had nothing to do with the amount of light or heat in the area. Our children expressed to us that they felt the same dark feelings and it would make them afraid, and uncomfortable in our new home. Previous owners had expressed that their kids had shared the same feelings with them.

We bought the house in late August, and by November I had been let go due to a past work-related injury. Now we had a new house that soon was facing foreclosure. So many negative things began to happen. My wife was feeling very depressed and alone, the kids didn't feel comfortable going downstairs alone, and my wife even felt a dark presence downstairs in the hall, laundry room and our bedroom, but she didn't express it to the kids for fear of upsetting them.

We stayed busy working with our church and growing in our faith. We volunteered for a program that helped homeless people. My wife and I were in the kitchen working on gathering scripture for a slide presentation. The kids were at the table eating breakfast. When they were finished, they left for school. A few moments later, the light fixture fell down from the ceiling onto the table in the exact spot where one of the children had been sitting. We felt we were being attacked.

We had noticed that every day there were several crows perched in our pine trees that were loud and annoying. The kids would caw back and chase them away but they would just come back. At the time we didn't realize the significance of the crows.

After a few months of the crows and strange feelings in the house, along with the foreclosure we were going through, I was prompted to ask my sister to pray for our family. During our conversation she recommended that she and a friend from her prayer group come over and pray with us for our home, land, and our financial situation. My sister explained to us that sin committed on our land could allow a curse to come upon the land and the house, and affect the people living there, even if they were Christians, and even if the sin was from long ago. My wife and I agreed to have them come over and pray with us.

During our meeting they shared with us the information in the book. "From God's Hands To Your Land". We prayed together to spiritually cleanse our house by repenting on behalf of any sin committed upon our property or in our home, and asked forgiveness. We asked that the blood of Jesus would set it free from all curses. We made plans to take communion, also know as the cup of redemption.

After my sister and her friend left, we immediately went out to a store and bought the items we needed to take communion. We came home and went into our back yard and did this. We felt so strongly not to let another night pass without completing what we knew we needed to do. After completing the ceremony, we felt that everything within the borders of our property had been washed clean by the blood of Jesus and that we would have a fresh start, free from any demonic entanglements; a clear spiritual title for our property. We had a confirmation within 24 hours of the prayer and communion.

The next afternoon we were out in the back yard thanking the Lord for what he had done for us. Suddenly we heard the crows coming for their regular afternoon social function, which was roosting in our trees and screaming at us and our house. I prayed that the Lord would send a predator to chase them away. Soon they flew into view, aiming straight for our yard. As they reached the front border of our property, we were amazed to see what happened. It was as if there was an invisible fence. They made an immediate turn, all together as if they were one, and went around our property to the neighbor's trees. At that same moment a red tailed hawk showed up and they all flew off, with him chasing them. Then four white doves appeared above our yard, and the crows were gone as fast as they came. The crows no longer hang out in our trees or on our property. Several months have gone by, and only one has tried. He was sitting on the corner of the property when we came home one day. My wife looked at him and said, "What do you think, you are doing here? You must leave!" and it flew away.

Since that evening there are no more dark or cold places in our home. The children sleep peacefully at night. On the night we all prayed together, Jeanette had explained about the Courtroom of Heaven and the legal rights that the enemy uses against us.

The Lord reminded me of a time in my past when I had been very angry one day about the way things were going in my life. I had called satan out, blaming him for the problems I was experiencing. My exact words to him were, "if you want a fight, I will give you a fight." The Lord reminded me of the exact location on the road that I had been driving on the day that I said those words of war. He showed me that I had opened a gate in my life that invited the enemy to come through, because of my angry words. This had caused me many problems, spiritually and physically.

It was a sin that I thought I could win a spiritual battle in the physical realm in my own strength. I knew better than this, but somehow my anger had blinded me. It was one of those instances like you see in the courtroom -- every word you say can and will be used against you. That is the truth.

After repenting, I felt a weight lift off of me. Several weeks later I was going to be driving through the area where I had challenged satan. I wanted to do something in the spiritual realm as a statement of completion and a symbol of reconciliation to the Lord. In faith I put anointing oil on my tires. As I was approaching the area I could see a bird flying towards me. As it got closer, I could see it was crow. I spoke to it and commanded it to leave in the name of Jesus, and that the gate to my life and family was closed. It made an immediate U-turn and left. Our family gives the Lord all the glory for all He has done for us. We simply believed His Word in faith and acted upon it.

The next week, out of the blue, we received a call from our Workman's Compensation lawyer. He said the insurance company had called and wanted to settle our claim. He wanted a figure for the amount of money that we would accept as a settlement. I gave him the same figure I had given at previous times. He wasn't optimistic but said he would get back with us. Within a week he called back and said they had accepted the figure and wanted to settle the case. The next week we received a call from the insurance company who had been paying on our vehicles while I was off work. They told me they were paying them off.

Many more life changing events have happened in our lives, but the most important thing we have learned is to be faithful to the Lord and He will direct your path and bless you.

The problem of a land-locked piece of property
Other symptoms of a curse might show up if you have felt led of the Lord to hold prayer meetings at your home and nothing seems to come together—people just keep having excuses why they can't make it to the meeting, even though they genuinely want to come. You could be dealing with a curse on the property that has it land-locked.

Property that is land-locked has no legal right-of-way of its own. It is surrounded by land or water or another person's property, with no gate of access. You have to gain permission to freely go back and forth across their property to get to yours. The enemy could have it locked up in the spiritual realm, which would mean he is possessing your gateway.

If the enemy has a legal hold on your property in some way, he will use that to hinder any type of activity that has to do with people meeting together to seek the Lord.

Counterfeit enactments can cause a curse on property

The enemy knows the importance of covenant enactments. People who are into the occult witchcraft realm often perform covenant rituals for their god. At some time in the history of the property, someone may have performed one of these enactments upon the land.

One example would be counterfeit drink offerings poured out to foreign gods in the past on your land, which would bring it under a curse.

> *And the Chaldean that fight against this city, shall come and set fire on this city, and burn it with the houses, upon whose roofs they have offered incense unto Baal, and poured out drink offerings unto other gods, to provoke me to anger.*
> *—Jeremiah. 32:29*

A person could be living on a piece of property that had at one time been dedicated to satan. It may have even had an altar to him on it. This would cause all kinds of problems for the people living on the land and they may not understand the significance of the sin upon the land. Sacrificing to a foreign god was, and still is. an abomination to the Lord.

Legal Rights for Renters

If you rent the property you are living in, you have an investment in that piece of real estate because you pay an amount of money each month to live there. Look at this money as seed you are sowing for a harvest of salvation for the person or company that you rent from.

You signed a lease and agreed to the rules. This means you have a legal right and responsibility to be the caretaker of what you are paying for each month. This entitles you to exercise authority over that piece of property.

The property might be blessed, but on the other hand it is possible that when you signed your rental agreement, you might have signed on with a spiritual demonic landlord that came with the property, who can cause you many different kinds of problems.

One person told me that she lived in a high-rise apartment, but was determined to dedicate and sanctify the land her apartment building was sitting on. She asked the Lord how she could do this, since there was concrete all around it.

She bought a pretty planter and filled it with soil that she purchased. She took communion and buried a copy of her lease in the planter. She then planted a plant in it as a memorial of fruitfulness. She wanted to make an altar, so she purchased one of those garden stones with a blessing on it and propped it up in front of the planter.

Scripture leaves no doubt there is a curse attached to the land when the blood of the righteous is shed on it.

Chapter 3
Purchasing A Curse

My personal experience of purchasing a curse
I was standing at the kitchen sink washing dishes, looking out of the window into the backyard. I suddenly burst into tears. I thought to myself, if I don't get some help I know I am going to go insane. I prayed to the Lord to help me overcome whatever it was that was happening to me.

For two weeks, after returning from a vacation, a feeling of despair and depression had begun to overtake me. I was helpless to stop it. I could hardly drag myself out of bed in the morning. This wasn't like me. I had a wonderful marriage and a six-month-old baby boy. My husband and I had begun to attend church after being away from the Lord for many years. Things couldn't have been better in my life. I had always been a happy person, never down. Life was always a laugh a minute.

I couldn't understand the heaviness and confusion of thoughts that had settled on me in the last two weeks.

That night before going to sleep, I asked my husband, Bud, to pray for me. Instead of asking the Lord to heal me, he asked the Lord to reveal to us what the problem was. The words had hardly left his mouth when a voice within me said "The blood of the righteous is crying up from the ground to Me for justice. You have bought and paid for a curse of insanity. I am a Righteous Judge and I have to render judgment against you."

This was a shock to me because I hadn't ever had the Lord speak to me; I felt doom and despair settle on me at His words of judgment. I told Bud what I had heard, and said, "What am I going to do? If I am under the judgment of God, who can help me?" Bud said, "Let's ask

Him what curse have we bought and paid for." As we asked, the Lord spoke again and said, "It is the gun you purchased while on vacation".

Two weeks earlier we had been in Michigan for a vacation and Bud had purchased an old gun as a collector's item. As I heard these words, I repeated them to Bud, and asked, "What kind of gun was it that you bought in Michigan?" He said, "It was a military sniper rifle."

I said, "It must have been used to kill righteous people. The person, or persons, who used it must have gone insane for the killings. I feel as if I am going insane. The curse came with the gun, and now it has come upon me. What are we going to do? Is there a way to be set free?"

Bud said, "We will pray a prayer of repentance for buying the gun. We will ask the Lord's forgiveness and pray that He will wash us and the gun with the blood of Jesus, and deliver us from the curse".

That is what we did. As soon as we completed the prayer, I physically felt something like a spider web come off of my head and shoulders. My mind was instantly clear and free. We praised and thanked the Lord for this supernatural deliverance. I asked the Lord where something like this is found in the Bible. I had never heard of such a thing. A few days later I came across this scripture in Genesis:

And the LORD said unto Cain, Where is Abel thy brother? And he said, I know not: Am I my brother's keeper? And he said, What hast thou done? the voice of thy brother's blood crieth unto me from the ground. And now art thou cursed from the earth, which hath opened her mouth to receive thy brother's blood from thy hand; When thou tillest the ground, it shall not henceforth yield unto thee her strength; a fugitive and a vagabond shalt thou be in the earth.. —Genesis 4:9-12

Scripture leaves no doubt there is a curse attached to the land when the blood of the righteous is shed on it. The Lord will avenge this blood. It is against His will to harm his children, but if the enemy can use the Word against us and get a judgment against our land or us, punishment has to be rendered.

The shed blood of Jesus on the cross paid the debt of the lien that the enemy may be holding against us and our land. As born again Christians, after repentance, we are entitled to claim the benefit of the shed blood of Jesus and apply it to the debt of sin.

It is a free gift for us, but we have to accept it and apply it to ourselves and our land. Like any gift, if you don't accept it you won't be able to enjoy the benefits of it.

When my children were teenagers, they were out scouting for a good site to camp a few blocks from where we lived. They came across a field where there had been a campfire. They had found a wood post with a cross nailed upside down to it. They found the remains of a dead cat and what looked like a bowl of urine. It was an important find because we hadn't been aware of witchcraft in the area. We prayed over the land, took the cross down and cleared the property of the other items. That piece of property had been for sale for a long time. After we prayed, it sold within weeks.

Years ago Bud was a part-time bee keeper. A good friend was also in this business. They had purchased bee hives from a place that was a few hours away from where we lived in Florida. The two of them went and picked up the hives, brought them home and delivered them around to our bee yards. That night as we were drifting off to sleep, suddenly I had a fearsome vision of arrows being shot, and spears being thrown at me. I immediately told Bud and we began to seek the Lord for the meaning of the vision.

As we were praying the vision changed. I saw our flatbed truck parked in front of our house with bee hives stacked on it, and on top of the bee hives were Indians painted with war paint. There weren't just a few Indians but appeared to be the whole Indian nation. They were standing row after row as far back as I could see. I think this meant the problem was from a long time ago. They were all in the offensive position, drawing back bows with arrows in them and holding up spears to throw at me.

My vision then swung around to the roofline of our house. On the roof were very tall angels, lined up shoulder to shoulder. Their wings were hanging down at their sides as if they were helpless to do anything about this attack.

I immediately told Bud what I was seeing. He said," I think we have bought and paid for a curse that has something to do with the Indians and the bee hives us and our friends who had also purchased bees hives. Immediately I had another vision. It was the bee truck with no Indians, just bee hives. In the vision, I saw the roof of our house and the angels. They had their arms up praising the Lord. We went right to sleep and had a peaceful night.

The next morning Bud called the man we had bought the bee hives from and asked him if they had any type of connection to Indians that he knew of. He said, "Yes, they were all on Indian burial mounds. Didn't you notice the hill they were on?"

Since then we have learned that the Indians consider their burial grounds to be sacred. Many tribes in the past, and maybe in the present, have a ceremony where they command a curse to come upon anyone who trespasses and disrupts the sanctity of the dead on their burial grounds.

*The Word says without repentance there
is no remission of sin, and since sin is
how the curse gained legal access to begin with,
it must be dealt with in the proper protocol of the Kingdom
of God to revoke and break it.*

Chapter 4

Breaking the Curse

As we repent, the Lord forgives and heals

We need to pray over the land, repenting on behalf of the sin that could have been committed on the land that would give a curse a legal right to come upon it.

> *When the heaven is shut up, and there is no rain, because they have sinned against thee; yet if they pray toward this place, and confess thy name, and <u>turn from their sin</u>, when thou dost afflict them; Then hear thou from heaven, and forgive the sin of thy servants, and of thy people Israel, when thou hast taught them the good way, wherein they should walk; and send rain upon thy land, which thou hast given unto thy people for an inheritance.*
> *—2 Chronicles 6:26-27 (emphasis added)*

To *turn* means to turn around, change your ways, and repent.

As you claim the land for the Lord, you will be investing seed, symbolically, for a crop of peace and righteousness. The divine light of truth springing forth from the ground will drive all demonic strongholds out. The Lord will move with mercy and grace in response to the truth of His Word when it is applied to set the land free. He who is righteous will look down from heaven and smile with favor upon us and our property.

> *Surely his salvation is nigh them that fear him; that glory may dwell in our land. Mercy and truth are met together; righteousness and peace have kissed each other. Truth shall spring out of the earth; and righteousness shall look down from heaven.* *—Psalm 85:9-11*

According to scripture, repentance comes before forgiveness. *Repentance* is the turning around of actions and hearts. It is an adjustment of a difference between us and God, and a restoration to favor. Restoration of the favor of God is given to sinners who repent and put their trust in the atoning death of Christ.

The Lord's Prayer says," Forgive us our sins as we forgive those who sin against us." (Luke 11:4) It is not only our sin that gets between us and God. It includes the visible or invisible sins that others may have committed that affect us. We need to ask for forgiveness for the sins we have committed, and then ask for forgiveness for those who sinned and allowed a curse to come. Since sin is how the curse gained legal access to begin with, sin must be dealt with in the proper protocol of the Kingdom of God to revoke and break the curse.

It is clear that to command that a curse be broken over a person or property in the name of Jesus, without first repenting, would omit the most important part. It is not enough to just say "curse be broken in the name of Jesus."

People ask if any Christian has authority to pray over a region that they might not even be from, and break the curses over it.

> *If My people, which are called by my name, shall humble themselves, and pray, and seek my face, and turn from their wicked ways; then will I hear from heaven, and will forgive their sin, and will heal their land.* −2 Chronicles 7:14

The scripture doesn't say that we have to be in a specific location to pray for the land for the Lord to heal it. The Lord instructs every believer, in Psalm 122:6, to "*pray for the peace of Jerusalem.*" He doesn't specify that you have to live in Jerusalem to do this. We see that when Aaron and Moses cursed the water of Egypt, and it all turned into blood, they were in one location but the water in *all* the land turned to blood.

The Lord says in James 5:16b, "*The effectual fervent prayer of a righteous man availeth much.*" *Effectual* means having adequate power or force to produce an effect. *Availeth* means to have strength or force to promote success or to answer a purpose. Any Christian, in any place, can be that 'righteous man' and be effective in prayer.

*The Lord uses
the heavens and the earth
as witnesses against the people for their sin.*

Chapter 5

The Courtroom of Heaven

The Courtroom of Heaven: how it pertains to our land

The scriptures speak about the Lord as the Righteous Judge of heaven and earth. The Bible teaches us that if we want to be blessed we need to live according to His laws or commandments. As we read the scriptures that pertain to the heavenly Courtroom setting, it is clear that the enemy petitions the Judge to obtain a judgment in the court of the Lord. This does have an impact upon our land on the earth. Little do most of us suspect that we, and our land, may be taking center stage daily in the Courtroom of Heaven.

I hope that as you read this information about the Courtroom in Heaven you will be empowered with the information necessary to win your case for complete victory of every battle here on the earth. We can use this strategy as a tool of intercession to clear the title deed of our property of spiritual liens. Here are the main participants in the Courtroom.

The Righteous Judge

The amount of scripture that describes the Lord as the Judge of heaven and earth are too numerous to include here. Here are a few examples.

> *The Lord takes his place in court; he rises to judge the people.*
> —*Isaiah 3:13 (NIV)*

> *Righteousness and justice are the foundation of His throne.*
> —*Psalm 97:2b (NIV)*

For we know him that hath said, Vengeance belongeth unto me, I will recompense, saith the Lord. And again, The Lord shall judge his people. —Hebrews 10:30

*For He is coming to judge the earth. With righteousness He shall judge the world, and the peoples with equity.
—Psalms 98:9*

The Lord is the Judge. If we place ourselves in that position we are in trouble. Don't get fooled into being an accuser, when we ourselves need a defender.

The following scriptures were addressed to believers.

But why dost thou judge thy brother? or why doest thou set at nought thy brother? For we shall all stand before the judgment seat of Christ. —Romans 14:10

There is one lawgiver, who is able to save and to destroy: who art thou that judgest another? —James 4:12

*For if ye forgive men their trespasses, your heavenly Father will also forgive you: But if ye forgive not men their trespasses, neither will your Father forgive your trespasses.
—Matthew 6:14-15*

*Judge not and yea shall not be judged: condemn not and ye shall not be condemned, forgive and ye shall be forgiven.
—Luke 6:37*

The Prosecuting Attorney - the accuser, satan

Day and night the enemy is presenting the evidence he has against us or our land in the Courtroom of Heaven. He seeks a guilty verdict so he can carry out the judgment against us.

*And I heard a loud voice saying in heaven, Now is come salvation, and strength, and the kingdom of our God, and the power of his Christ: for the accuser of our brethren is cast down, which accused them before our God day and night.
—Revelations 12:10*

He has to go to the Judge to get the right to prosecute us (see Job 1), unless he already has a case open against us. Because our God has established the foundations of His earth on righteousness and justice, the enemy can present evidence of sin committed on our land and win a guilty verdict against it and us. He would gain the order from the Judge to execute the judgment written against us because of the testimony of the sin. Sin restricts the Lord's hand of blessing on the land unless and until the debts are paid in full and it once again has a clear title deed.

In a time of emotional upset we might mistakenly address the prosecuting attorney, demanding things of him that he isn't capable of doing. It would be a waste of our time to argue our case with our spiritual enemy. He hopes to entangle us in this useless pastime. It could be possible that, by the words of our mouth, it would appear to the Lord that we are giving the devil more credit than he deserves.

There is courtroom protocol that has to be followed. In the courtroom on the earth, we wouldn't be addressing the prosecuting attorney in our defense. The Judge is the one who can pardon or convict us. His decision is based upon the evidence presented. Throughout scripture we see testimony of the Lord as the Righteous Judge, executing judgment.

He is the one with all authority over every dominion or principality that rules over the earth.

> *...above all principality, and power, and might, and dominion, and every name that is named, not only in this world, but also in that which is to come.* —Ephesians 1:21

The Witnesses

The Lord uses the heavens and the earth as witnesses against the people for their sin.

> *I call heaven and earth to record this day against you, that I have set before you life and death, blessing and cursing; therefore choose life that both thou and thy seed may live.* —Deuteronomy 30:19

> *If thou shalt keep all these commandments to do them, which I command thee this day, to love the LORD thy God, and to walk ever in his ways; then shalt thou add three cities more for thee, beside these three: That innocent blood be not shed in thy land, which the LORD thy God giveth thee for an inheritance, and so blood be upon thee.* —Deuteronomy 19: 9-10

> *I call heaven and earth to witness against you this day, that ye shall soon utterly perish from off the land whereunto ye go over Jordan to possess it; ye shall not prolong your days upon it, but shall utterly be destroyed.* —Deuteronomy 4:26

The heavens witness by withholding the rain. The earth testifies to the curse by the fact that it can't produce a crop without the rain. Today it isn't a matter of life or death if people can't grow a crop on their land. But in ancient Bible days, without rain to make crops grow, they may have starved to death.

> *Wherefore seeing we also are compassed about with so great a cloud of witnesses, let us lay aside every weight, and the sin which doth so easily beset us, and let us run with patience the race that is set before us.   —Hebrews 12:1*

Our personal testimony is our witness. It is evidence that can be used in our favor or against us.

> *For our rejoicing is this, the testimony of our conscience, that in simplicity and godly sincerity, not with fleshly wisdom, but by the grace of God, we have had our conversation in the world, and more abundantly to you-ward. —2 Corinthians 1:12*

> *Even now, behold, my witness is in heaven, and he who vouches for me is on high.   —Job 16:19*

The Court Recorder

In the vision of Ezekiel, he saw a spirit being who was in charge of records, marking people who were the intercessors for the city who would be spared during the time of the Lord's wrath.

> *And behold, six men came from the direction of the upper gate, which faces north, every man with His battle-ax in his hand; and one man among them was clothed in linen, with writer's ink bottle at his side....And he called to the man clothed with linen, which had the writer's inkhorn by his side; And the LORD said unto him, Go through the midst of the city, through the midst of Jerusalem, and set a mark upon the foreheads of the men that sigh and that cry for all the abominations that be done in the midst thereof.*
> *—Ezekiel 9:2-4*

Heaven and earth watch, listen, and write our words and deeds.

> *Gather unto me all the elders of your tribes, and your officers, that I may speak these words in their ears, and call heaven and earth to record against them. —Deuteronomy 31: 28*

> *Then they that feared the LORD spake often one to another: and the LORD hearkened, and heard it, and a book of remembrance was written before him for them that feared the LORD, and that thought upon his name. —Malachi 3:16*

And I saw the dead, small and great, stand before God; and the books were opened: and another book was opened, which is [the book] of life: and the dead were judged out of those things which were written in the books, according to their works. —Revelations 20:12

*The Lord wants to
rename our property
so His blessings will flow
in a greater measure*

Chapter 6
A New Name

Land is alive and needs to be set free

Scripture tells us just how alive the land is. The land is responsive. It can be joyful.

> *Let the heavens rejoice, and let the earth be glad; let the sea roar, and the fullness thereof. --Psalm 96:11*

The land has a mouth and it can drink.

> *And now art thou cursed from the earth, which hath opened her mouth to receive thy brother's blood from thy hand. —Genesis 4:11*

> *Thou stretchedst out thy right hand, the earth swallowed them. —Exodus 15:12*

> *But if the LORD make a new thing, and the earth open her mouth, and swallow them up, with all that appertain unto them, and they go down quick into the pit; then ye shall understand that these men have provoked the LORD....And the earth opened her mouth, and swallowed them up, and their houses, and all the men that appertained unto Korah, and all their goods. —Numbers 16:30,32*

It can be sad and vomit.

> *And the land is defiled: therefore I do visit the iniquity thereof upon it, and the land itself vomiteth out her inhabitants. – Leviticus 18:25*

The earth has ears; it can hear.

> *Hear O heavens, and give ear, O earth: for the Lord hath spoken. I have nourished and brought up children, and they have rebelled against me. --Isaiah 1:2*

A testimony about life coming from the land

My name is Melissa Powell, and I have two testimonies concerning "Redeeming the Land". The first one is a vision the Lord gave me as I was reading a person's account of going to heaven for a short period of time. One of the things she said was that when she stepped on the grass in heaven, she felt energy go through her body from the life coming from it. The Lord showed me that when our land is under the curse, it drains our energy and vitality. When we share communion with the land and redeem it, there is energy and vitality coming up from the earth to us.

The second testimony concerns my aunt. She had received a large settlement in her divorce and wanted to have a place for our family of eight sisters and their husbands and kids, to be able to relax and enjoy each other. She bought 70 acres of wooded and fielded land behind my grandparents' 70-acre farm. She put it in the names of all of her sisters and herself. She is a very smart and savvy businesswoman so she put the property into an LLC, which is a "Limited Liability Corporation". If something unforeseen happened on the land, the liability would be covered by the corporation. The intention was to put my grandparents' farm in the LLC when the time came so it would stay in the family. My mom is the eldest of the sisters, and being one of the names on the title deed, she had the authority to have communion with the land and to give it a new spiritual title.

Jeanette and another of the women from her prayer group came out, and the four of us performed the Land Redemption Ceremony. We didn't notice a big change the summer we did it. But the following summer we did begin to see a remarkable difference. Before we had the ceremony, there were so many coyotes on the land that we never saw small animals like rabbits or squirrels. The following summer we started noticing them. It is like the woods came to life. We also noticed the small animals on my grandfather's farm. We have since learned that he had put his farm in the LLC when he was having several operations for a blood clot in his leg, so his farm and land was also redeemed at the same time. I am so grateful and thankful the Lord is running the show!

I had shared part of this testimony at one of our prayer meetings at Jeanette's. She asked if I would like to share the testimony in this book. The Lord began to show me the things that have happened since we had communion with the land.

41

Many family truths have been coming to light and are still coming to light. It may not seem wonderful at the time, but when family secrets come to light there can be repentance and healing, and curses can be broken. Some of those truths started coming to light last summer. I didn't realize at the time why it was happening. I attribute this to my grandfathers' land being redeemed. I believe my family is beginning to heal.

The other thing I remember is that before the Land Redemption Ceremony, we always called the land "The LLC." It wasn't a conscious decision, but in the last year we began to call it the "River Park". The Lord Himself renamed our property. He wants to rename yours, too.

The Lord wants to rename our property so His blessings will flow in a greater measure

Names are very important to the Lord. We see Him change names many times in the Bible so the person, water well, or land could move into its prophetic position of becoming a memorial to Him, as a testimony of what He had done.

He has names for everything created, even the stars in the Heavens.

> *Look up into the heavens. Who created all the stars? He brings them out one after another, calling each by its name. And he counts them to see that none are lost or have strayed away.*
> *—Isaiah. 40:26 (NLT)*

Here are sample names you can choose from, or to use to get your creative ideas flowing.

The High Gate, Vineyard Gate, Floral Garden, Heavens Gate, Garden Gate, House of Praise, House of Prayer, The Home of Uplifted Praise, Gracious Provision, Garden of God, Beulah, Gate of Blessing, Glory, Freedom, Heaven, Abundant Acres, High Places, High Hills, Hidden Treasure Farm, Quiet Meadows, Peaceful, Tranquil.

Before or after any of these names you could put other words such as: Farm, River, Ranch, Hill, Valley, Estate, Home, Lake or Stream.

Scriptural examples of name changes for land

FOR ZION'S sake will I Isaiah not hold my peace, and for Jerusalem's sake I will not rest until her imputed righteousness and vindication go forth as brightness, and her salvation radiates, as does a burning torch ²And the nations shall see your righteousness and vindication your rightness and justice-- not your own, but His ascribed to you, and all kings shall behold your salvation and glory; and you shall be called by a new name, which the mouth of the Lord shall name. ³You shall also be so beautiful and prosperous as to be thought of as a crown of glory and honor in the hand of the Lord, and a royal diadem exceedingly beautiful in the hand of your God. ⁴You Judah shall no more be termed Forsaken, nor shall your land be called Desolate any more. But you shall be called Hephzibah My delight is in her and your land be called Beulah married; for the Lord delights in you, and your land shall be married owned and protected by the Lord. ⁵For as a young man marries a virgin O Jerusalem, so shall your sons marry you; and as the bridegroom rejoices over the bride, so shall your God rejoice over you.   —Isaiah 62:1-5 (AMP)   (emphasis added)

And Isaac digged again the wells of water, which they had digged in the days of Abraham, his father; for the Philistines had stopped them after the death of Abraham: and he called their names after the names by which his father had called them. —Genesis 26:18

This symbolic enactment of establishing a New Covenant and the naming of your land is recorded in Heaven.

Then they that feared the Lord spoke often one to another, and the Lord hearkened, and heard it, and a book of remembrance was written before Him for them that feared the Lord, and that thought upon His name. —Malachi 3: 16

The Lord is listening and watching our activities. This is one activity that brings Him great joy. We are doing exploits for His kingdom.

Your Title Deed

A *Title Deed* is a written instrument that is signed and delivered by which one individual, the grantor, conveys title to real property to another individual, the grantee; it is a conveyance of land, tenements, or hereditaments, from one individual to another.

In Common Law, a deed was an instrument under seal that contained a covenant or contract delivered by the individual who was to be bound by it, to the party to whom it was granted. It can also symbolize a prophetic statement of release of lien in the natural.

In Habakkuk 2:11, the Lord says to write the vision and make it clear. If He has given you a vision of a payoff of your mortgage, write it down. In faith you are decreeing the payoff of your mortgage.

On the next page you will find a symbolic new Title Deed that you can copy or tear out of the book, fill in the blanks, then bury as part of this ceremony. You might want to frame a copy as a memorial to the day of your land's new birth. Another copy is included as an addendum at the end of the book.

The title will be a visible symbolic witness for the Court of Law of heaven and earth. On this title deed you can give your piece of property a new spiritual name.

Below is what is written on your title deed. We have included it in this way because the print is so small on the picture of the deed itself. You could also use this wording to create your own version. This Title Deed shows that the land is free and clear of any spiritual liens, and shows the Lord as the owner.

Title Deed

To all parties with any interest in the land formally known as:

(Address) _____.

It will be known as_____. (Prophetic name)

This land is now, and shall remain free from any ungodly spiritual encumbrances or liens of any kind from this day thru eternity, because of the saving grace of the shed blood of Jesus Christ.

This deed is hereby freely transferred to Jehovah God, The Creator of Heaven and Earth, as a clear title.

Witness_____ Date_____
Witness_____ Date_____

The seal says: *The official seal of God the Father, Jesus Christ the Son, and the Holy Spirit.*

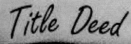

Title Deed

To all parties with any interest in the land formally known as (address)

_____

It will be known as _____

This land is now, and shall remain free from any ungodly spiritual encumbrances or liens of the kind from this day through eternity, because of the saving grace of the shed blood of Jesus Christ

The land is hereby freely transferred to Jehovah God with a clear title

Witness _____

Date _____

Witness _____

Date _____

OFFICIAL SEAL
PAID IN FULL
BY THE BLOOD

From God's Hands to your land

*We are using
the Courtroom of Heaven
and the laws of God to set our land free.*

Chapter 7
Reestablishing Covenant

The beautiful ceremony we perform, as a symbolic sign of renewal of vows between our land and its Lord, demonstrates a covenant marriage between the Lord and the land, and a divorce from the sin and worship of foreign gods.

> *Thou shalt no more be termed Forsaken; neither shall thy land any more be termed Desolate: but thou shalt be called Hephzibah, and thy land Beulah: for the LORD delighteth in thee, and thy land shall be married.* —Isaiah 62:4

Part of this ceremony includes the taking of the cup and the bread of remembrance (communion), and the building of an altar or memorial.

The cup and the bread of remembrance
Partaking of the cup and the bread of remembrance with the land is an act of faith, an outward symbol or testimony of restoration and reconciliation of the land to the Lord.

It could be considered a memorial of His goodness and mercy on behalf of the land, clearing the title of all liens against it.

> *NOW FAITH is the assurance the confirmation, the title deed of the things we hope for, being the proof of things we do not see and the conviction of their reality faith perceiving as real fact what is not revealed to the senses For by faith trust and holy fervor born of faith the men of old had divine testimony borne to them and obtained a good report. By faith we understand that the worlds during the successive ages] were framed fashioned, put in order, and equipped for their intended purpose by the word of God, so that what we see was not made out of things which are visible.* —Hebrews 11:1-3 (AMP)

Some might ask, "Do we need to actually take part in a Covenant of Redemption Ceremony with our land? If we pray over it, will it work the same?" There are many examples in the Word where the Lord required an action and a blood sacrifice to redeem the people and give them back their land from the hands of the enemy.

The story of Gideon, as found in Judges, is just one example of many. Judges 5:31 is the beginning of the story. It begins by saying that the Lord was on the side of the Israelites because they worshipped Him and obeyed His commandments. Scripture says that, as a reward, their land had rest for forty years. But then we see in Judges 6:1:

> *The children of Israel did evil in the sight of the LORD: and the LORD delivered them into the hand of Midian seven years.*

The land and the people came under the bondage of their enemies because of the sin they committed against God. They lost their crops and other provisions. After seven years, the people cried out to the Lord.

> *And there came an angel of the LORD, and sat under an oak, which was in Ophrah, that pertained unto Joash the Abiezrite: and his son Gideon threshed wheat by the winepress, to hide it from the Midianites.*
>
> *And the angel of the LORD appeared unto him, and said unto him, The LORD is with thee, thou mighty man of valour. And Gideon said unto him, Oh my Lord, if the LORD be with us, why then is all this befallen us? And where be all his miracles, which our fathers told us of, saying, did not the LORD bring us up from Egypt? But now the LORD hath forsaken us, and delivered us into the hands of the Midianites. And he said unto him, if now I have found grace in thy sight, then shew me a sign that thou talkest with me. Depart not hence, I pray thee, until I come unto thee, and bring forth my present, and set it before thee.*
>
> *And he said, I will tarry until thou come again. And the LORD said unto him, surely I will be with thee, and thou shalt smite the Midianites as one man. And Gideon went in, and made ready a kid, and unleavened cakes of an ephah of flour: the flesh he put in a basket, and he put the broth in a pot, and brought it out unto him under the oak, and presented it. And the angel of God said unto him, Take the flesh and the unleavened cakes, and lay them upon this rock, and pour out the broth. And he did so.*
>
> *Then the angel of the LORD put forth the end of the staff that was in his hand, and touched the flesh and the unleavened*

cakes; and there rose up fire out of the rock, and consumed the flesh and the unleavened cakes. Then the angel of the LORD departed out of his sight. –Judges 6:2-21

The first offering that Gideon prepared was a sacrifice for his personal sins. The angel of the Lord accepted the offering.

Then the Lord said to him, "Peace be with you; do not fear, you shall not die." —vs. 23

Gideon built an altar of memorial as a visible testimony of the Word of the Lord given to him.

Then Gideon built an altar there unto the LORD, and called it Jehovah shalom: unto this day it is yet in Ophrah of the Abiezrites. —vs. 24

God instructed Gideon to offer another blood sacrifice. He told Gideon to tear down the altars to the foreign gods that his generational bloodline and the townspeople worshipped, and sacrifice a bull. This was the sacrifice on behalf of the people and the land.

And it came to pass the same night, that the LORD said unto him, Take thy father's young bullock, even the second bullock of seven years old, and throw down the altar of Baal that thy father hath, and cut down the grove that is by it: And build an altar unto the LORD thy God upon the top of this rock, in the ordered place, and take the second bullock, and offer a burnt sacrifice with the wood of the grove which thou shalt cut down. —vs. 25-26

Altars to foreign gods were usually built near a grove of trees for the convenience of a firewood supply needed for the burnt sacrifices. God instructed them to cut down the poles of Baal, which were altar poles, and burn up the wood. The Lord was making a statement to the principalities and powers, and He was using man to do this. Men are God's hands on the earth.

Then Gideon took ten men of his servants, and did as the LORD had said unto him: and so it was, because he feared his father's household, and the men of the city, that he could not do it by day, that he did it by night. And when the men of the city arose early in the morning, behold, the altar of Baal was cast down, and the grove was cut down that was by it, and the second bullock was offered upon the altar that was built. And they said one to another, who hath done this thing? And when they enquired and asked, they said, Gideon the son of Joash hath done this thing. Then the men of the city said unto Joash,

Bring out thy son, that he may die: because he hath cast down the altar of Baal, and because he hath cut down the grove that was by it. And Joash said unto all that stood against him, Will ye plead for Baal, will ye save him? He that will plead for him, let him be put to death whilst it is yet morning: if he be a god, let him plead for himself, because one hath cast down his altar. Therefore on that day he called him Jerubbaal, saying, Let Baal plead against him, because he hath thrown down his altar....But the Spirit of the LORD came upon Gideon, and he blew a trumpet; and Abiezer was gathered after him.
—Judges 6:27-32, 34

The blowing of the trumpet (shofar), which is a ram's horn, was the signal to the heavenly host to be prepared to fight the ensuing battle on behalf of the Israelites. In Hebrew this scripture literally says "The Spirit of the Lord clothed himself with Gideon," which means, "He took possession of Gideon."

The rest of the story tells how the Lord delivered Israel's enemies into their hands. They won their battle and took back the land.

An important thing to note in this story is that to redeem the people and get back possession of their land, they had to offer a sacrifice or blood offering for the sin, as directed by the Lord. Gideon had to physically do something as an offering of repentance and thanksgiving.

Today there is a spiritual birthing of a new initiative to take back the land for the Lord. The goal is restoration for land transformation.

Within this spiritual initiative of the Lord that is being enacted in the physical are at least three objectives

An *initiative* is a process by which laws may be introduced or enacted directly by vote of the people. We are utilizing the Courtroom of heaven and the laws of God to set our land free.

1. Reclamation: Make new again; recover; to bring back from error; to make wasteland usable.

2. Reformation: To make better as by stopping abuses; to cause to behave better; reforming.

3. Restoration: Restoring or being restored; something restored as by re-building; to give back.

We perform the physical act of the Covenant of Remembrance Ceremony with the land, as a witness between heaven and earth of our covenant relationship with the Lord God of heaven and earth.

Our salvation won't be affected if we don't take part in a Covenant of Remembrance ceremony with our land. However, we may also not enjoy the physical changes that we could experience when we allow our land to take of the cleansing bread and blood of Jesus that will give it victory, rest, and peace.

> And the tree of the field shall yield her fruit, and the earth shall yield her increase, and they shall be safe in their land, and shall know that I am the LORD, when I have broken the bands of their yoke, and delivered them out of the hand of those that served themselves of them. –Ezekiel 34:27

The significance of altars

The Covenant of Remembrance Ceremony that is described at the end of this book recommends the building of an altar to the Lord upon the site. For those who would choose to call it something else it could be called a memorial. It will be a visible sign that symbolizes a memorial to the Lord for what He has done for us.

Generally altars function as sacrificial platforms. Their construction can also mark the introduction of the worship of a particular god in a new land. One tie between the generations of covenantal leaders is their construction of altars in order to worship Yahweh in the Promised Land.

There are several examples of the naming of memorial altars:

> And Jacob went out from Beersheba, and went toward Haran. And he lighted upon a certain place, and tarried there all night, because the sun was set; and he took of the stones of that place, and put them for his pillows, and lay down in that place to sleep. And he dreamed, and behold a ladder set up on the earth, and the top of it reached to heaven: and behold the angels of God ascending and descending on it.
>
> And, behold, the LORD stood above it, and said, I am the LORD God of Abraham thy father, and the God of Isaac: the land whereon thou liest, to thee will I give it, and to thy seed; And thy seed shall be as the dust of the earth, and thou shalt spread abroad to the west, and to the east, and to the north, and to the south: and in thee and in thy seed shall all the families of the earth be blessed.

And, behold, I [am] with thee, and will keep thee in all [places] whither thou goest, and will bring thee again into this land; for I will not leave thee, until I have done that which I have spoken to thee of.

And Jacob awaked out of his sleep, and he said, surely the LORD is in this place; and I knew it not. And he was afraid, and said, how dreadful is this place! This is none other but the house of God, and this is the gate of heaven. And Jacob rose up early in the morning, and took the stone that he had put for his pillows, and set it up for a pillar, and poured oil upon the top of it. And he called the name of that place Bethel: but the name of that city was called Luz at the first.
—Genesis 28:10-19

He re-titled the location by giving it a new name. Jacob associated God with the place where he had the dream. He memorialized it with the stone at his head and consecrated it with oil.

The altar Moses builds is one of commemoration of the victory (Exodus 17:15). The name given it, "Yahweh is my Standard," reflects the theology of Yahweh as the leader of the armies of Israel. In the Egyptian army the divisions were named for various gods (e.g., the division of Amun, division of Seth) and the standards would identify the division by means of some representation of the god. (WORD Search Bible Background Commentary)

An altar can be used as a symbol or witness of a dedication

Joshua 4 tells the story of the children of Israel crossing over the Jordan River into the Promised Land and, as the Lord directed, marking that historic crossing over with a memorial of remembrance with stones.

Take for yourselves twelve men from the people, one man from every tribe, and command them saying, "Take for yourselves twelve stones from here, out of the midst of the Jordan, from the place where the priests feet stood firm. You shall carry them over with you and leave them in the lodging place where you lodge tonight. that this may be a sign among you when your children ask in time to come, saying, "What do these stones mean to you?" Then you shall answer them that the waters of the Jordan were cut off before the Ark of the Covenant of the Lord; when it crossed over the Jordan, the waters of the Jordan were cut off. And these stones shall be for a memorial to the children of Israel forever.
—Joshua 4:2-6, 6-7

Joshua 22, starting at verse 10 through the end of the chapter, is a very interesting story. It appears the Israelites had a discussion about building an altar as a witness or memorial, instead of an altar for sacrifice only. The two-and-a-half tribes that had stayed on one side of the Jordan had built an altar. The rest of the Israelites thought they were in rebellion and had committed a breach of faith against God. The tribes that built the altar explained to Phinehas, the priest, that their altar was not for burnt offering or for sacrifice, but to be a witness between them and the generations after them, that they would perform the service of the Lord only in His presence in Jerusalem. (Judges 22:26-27). The text goes on to say that they called the altar "Witness", for it was to be a witness between them that the LORD is God. The explanation satisfied the priest and the heads of the congregation.

The next place we see the site of a memorial is in Joshua 24:27.

> And Joshua said unto all the people, Behold, this stone shall
> be a witness unto us; for it hath heard all the words of the
> LORD which he spake unto us: it shall be therefore a witness
> unto you, lest ye deny your God.

If a person doesn't feel comfortable with the act or term of building an altar with stones on the site of the covenant ceremony, it could be called a stone of memorial or remembrance. It represents the place where the Lord removed the curse and once again became the title deed owner of the property, and that all curses or liens in the spiritual realm have been legally cleared from the title.

Is the act of pouring Salt on land, a symbol of covenant?

Many people have asked about pouring salt on their land as a symbol of covenant with the Lord. They presume it is a sign of blessing, when it may not be. The scripture speaks of salt 41 times in 35 different verses. It seems that when the scripture speaks of salt on land it is a negative.

The Dictionary of Biblical Imagery says Jesus contrasts salt's positive and negative potential:

> You are the salt of the earth; but if the salt has become
> tasteless, how will it be made salty again? It is good for
> nothing any more. —Matthew 5:13 (NASV)

The Salt Sea (Dead Sea), the Valley of Salt and the City of Salt all connote death, desolation, despair and desert.

> *And that the whole land thereof is brimstone, and salt, and burning, that it is not sown, nor beareth, nor any grass groweth therein, like the overthrow of Sodom, and Gomorrah, Admah, and Zeboim, which the LORD overthrew in his anger, and in his wrath.* —Deuteronomy 29:23

To Abimelech, spreading salt on a captured city symbolized a curse:

> *And Abimelech fought against the city all that day; and he took the city, and slew the people that was therein, and beat down the city, and sowed it with salt.* —Judges 9:45

> *For he shall be like the heath in the desert, and shall not see when good cometh; but shall inhabit the parched places in the wilderness, a salt land and not inhabited.* —Jeremiah 17:6

If salt is poured on plant it will die. My husband took a container of salt and poured it on some grass along the roadway. Within a few days the grass died.

> *But the miry places thereof and the marshes thereof shall not be healed; they shall be given to salt.* -- Ezekiel 47:11

> *Can the fig tree, my brethren, bear olive berries? Either a vine, figs? so can no fountain both yield salt water and fresh.* —James 3:12

When Elisha threw the salt into the water at Jericho, it served to reverse the curse that Joshua had charged it with. This is an example of a curse having staying power until it is broken. It was a sign and a wonder to encourage the people that God was with them.

Here is another example of salt being put into water but there is no of putting it on land.

> *And he said, bring me a new cruse, and put salt therein. And they brought it to him. And he went forth unto the spring of the waters, and cast the salt in there, and said, thus saith the LORD, I have healed these waters; there shall not be from thence any more death or barren.* —2 Kings 2:20-21

(Some versions add *land* to the end and some don't.)

To include the salt in your ceremony is between you and the Lord. He might tell you to pour salt. I am not saying that if someone has poured salt on his or her land in the past that it was wrong. Pray and see if it is what the Lord wants.

I talked to a woman who told me that there was a curse on her property so she prayed and poured salt all around the borders of her property. When I asker her why she did this she said that it was all over in the Bible to do that, and a pastor had told her to do it. She said that demons would see it and they wouldn't come on her property.

It is important to search for information for ourselves about this subject of pouring salt on the land as a sign of covenant. I welcome any additional comments about pouring salt on land as a sign of covenant with God.

*The redeeming of the Land
is an act of war in the spiritual realm.*

Chapter 8
Needed elements

These are the things you will need for the Covenant of Remembrance Ceremony: The Ceremony usually takes about 15 minutes.

▫ a shovel or other digging tool
▫ grape juice or wine,
▫ bread
▫ oil
▫ water
▫ milk
▫ honey
▫ corn, wheat or another symbol of crop
▫ your symbolic Title Deed completed, including the new prophetic name
▫ a watertight container in which to place the Title Deed
        (it could be as simple as a plastic bag)

Other items you may want:
▫ a rock or other item for an altar or memorial
▫ a shofar (if you have one available)
▫ a map of the area you are praying over
▫ CD player and worship music
▫ banner

A "Land Kit" is available that includes much of what you need for this ceremony. Each kit includes flower seeds and heirloom vegetable seeds, as well as other crop seeds such as corn, wheat, barley etc. These all speak of the restoration of the earth to the time the Lord created the Garden of Eden, the time of the original clear title deed. The seeds symbolically come with a promise of fruitfulness for our ground.

And God said, Behold, I have given you every herb bearing seed, which is upon the face of all the earth, and every tree, in the which is the fruit of a tree yielding seed; to you it shall be for meat. —Genesis 1: 29

He that goeth forth and weepeth, bearing precious seed, shall doubtless come again with rejoicing, bringing his sheaves with him. —Psalm 126:6

The symbol of seed in this particular scripture points back to the root word for human reproduction. We are symbolically saying our generational seed will be productive for the Kingdom of God and bring forth a harvest of salvations.

The Lord may have you bring other items to put in the ground. Some people have given testimony of burying a wedding ring, the type you can pick up at a local variety store. They quote this scripture for that.

Thou shalt no more be termed Forsaken; neither shall thy land any more be called Desolate: but thou shalt be called Hepzibah, and thy land Beulah: for the Lord delighteth in thee, and thy land shall be married. —Isaiah 62:4 (NASV)

You may want to include a map of the borders of the area or region you are claiming for the Lord. If it is a city, then a map of the city limits would be good. For property you live on, own, or rent, show the boundaries in the rental or purchase agreement.

Plan for something permanent to mark the spot where you are burying the Title Deed. You can use one or more rocks. It's not necessarily the size of the rock or rocks, unless the Lord specifically says so. It is the symbol that is important.

You may also want a shofar to blow, symbolizing the presence of the Lord. The redeeming of the Land is an act of war in the spiritual realm. The enemy may have had control of our land, but we are taking it back for the Lord. It is coming under the dominion of the Lord.

The blowing of the shofar will alert the heavenly host to come for the battle. As we take care of the legal issues that have held the land in spiritual and physical bondage, the Heavenly Host will come and defeat our enemies who have held it captive.

When you go to war in your land against the enemy who oppresses you, then you shall sound an alarm with the trumpets, and you will be remembered before the Lord your God, and you will be saved from your enemies. —Numbers 10:9

If you don't have a shofar, raise your voice like a shofar.

> *Cry aloud, spare not, lift up thy voice like a trumpet, and shew my people their transgression, and the house of Jacob their sins. —Isaiah 58:1*

In ancient days the shofar was blown at the dethroning of kings and the enthroning of a new king. We are dethroning principalities, stripping them of their power over our land, and enthroning the Lord of the Host. We use it to celebrate the Divine Exchange—from curse to blessing.

As we are in a state of repentance on behalf of sin, the Lord hears the cry and responds to a repentant heart. Blow the shofar, or lift up your voice as a shofar, at the very beginning of the ceremony and again at the end.

Prepare the ground by digging a small hole or short furrow
The size and depth to dig will be according to the items that you plan to bury.

It is possible that you may feel led of the Holy Spirit to remove your shoes or kneel down during the following prayers and decrees. Be sensitive to what the Lord is saying for you to do.

As you dig the hole, consider it to be a symbolic well, a well that will bring forth reclamation, reformation and restoration. Some dig a hole in the immediate area around the wellhead on their property, or in the area where the water lines come into the building.

> *And he builded an altar there, and called upon the name of the LORD, and pitched his tent there: and there Isaac's servants digged a well. —Genesis 26:25*

Justice for our land through reconciliation

Chapter 9

Covenant of Remembrance Ceremony

Step 1. Prayers of reconciliation and repentance

If you are covenanting the land by yourself then speak the prayers, and decrees in the first person saying *I*, instead of *we*.

> *Sow to yourselves in righteousness, reap in mercy; break up your fallow ground: for it is time to seek the LORD, till he come and rain righteousness upon you.* —Hosea 10:12

Foundation prayer for personal reconciliation:

> Father of heaven and earth, Creator of the universe, we humbly come before You this day to make intercession, first on behalf of ourselves, then on behalf of our land. As we humbly stand before You, the Righteous Judge of Heaven and Earth, presenting our case, we repent on behalf of any sin that we or anyone in our generational bloodline have committed against You. We renounce all sin, and ask Your forgiveness for that sin. We ask that You would move any case the enemy has against us from the Courtroom of Judgment to the Throne Room of Grace, for a season of grace and mercy, and to remove any veil that has been over the eyes of our understanding that has prevented us from understanding and embracing Your truth in every area

of our lives. We ask that You extend grace and mercy to us as we come into alignment with Your perfect will for our lives.

We present ourselves before You as a freewill offering, just as You became a freewill offering for us, to redeem us from our sins through the shedding of Your blood on the cross. We acknowledge that it is Your shed blood that sets us free from our sins. We decree that You alone are on the altar of our hearts. Amen.

Prayer of repentance and reconciliation on behalf of sin committed upon the land

Father, we come into the Courtroom of Heaven as Your Kingdom children. We stand before You as the Righteous Judge of Heaven and Earth. We are here to present an appeal in the case that the enemy may have against our land. We understand that he is using the testimony and evidence of sin committed upon the land to obtain a judgment against it. We come humbly and respectfully before You as ambassadors of reconciliation on behalf of our land. We stand in the gap, repenting on behalf of sin that has been committed against You on this land.

We ask that this record go back to the earliest days of this land's birth, when You laid its' original foundations. We thank You that, as we humbly seek You in repentance, You will remove all old covenants of sin. As we repent and ask Your forgiveness for the sin, You say in Your Word You will be faithful to forgive.We ask that You cleanse our land by Your blood, removing all curses and judgments, so that this land can be released into a season of grace and mercy.

We dedicate our land to You, so that the prophetic destiny You have planned for this land since the beginning of creation will come to pass. As we pray in this way, we thank You that there has been justice decreed on behalf of this land in the Courtroom of Heaven. There shall be a physical manifestation on the earth concerning this land. Amen.

Step 2. The Bread - a symbol of the Body of Jesus

Each person is to take a piece of bread, or whatever you are going to use to symbolize the body of Christ. Break it in two pieces, one for yourself and one for the land. (This can be done other ways, in whatever way the Holy Spirit directs you.) Don't eat the bread yet.

Prayer of declaration before the bread is eaten
Everyone can pray this prayer and quote the scripture in unity.

> *Our Father which art in heaven, Hallowed be thy name. Thy kingdom come. Thy will be done, in earth as it is in heaven. Give us this day our daily bread, forgive us our debts, as we forgive our debtors. Do not lead us not into temptation; but deliver us from the evil one. For yours is the Kingdom, and the Power and the Glory forever. Amen.* —Matthew 6:9

The leader decrees:

> *Jesus said: "I am the living bread, which came down from heaven: if any man eats of this bread, he shall live forever: and the bread that I will give is my flesh, which I will give for the life of the world." —John 6:51*

We declare that this bread represents the body of Christ that was given for us as a sacrifice for our sin. The bread of heaven, sent to earth to bring reconciliation and healing. We ask that as we eat of this bread and place it in the mouth of our land, it will bring nourishment and restoration. We consecrate this land to provision and abundance. We declare that it will be nourished with the hidden manna of righteousness, peace and joy. Amen

Eat your portion and place the other half in the ground.

Step 3. Partake of the cup of remembrance of the covenant

The leader decrees:

> Jesus Christ has chosen believers to be His ambassadors or representatives for Him on the earth. (2 Corinthians 5:20) As

such, we have been given legal "Power of Attorney" to apply His blood to sin that has been atoned for and reconciled, through repentance and forgiveness. This is the 'blood for blood' required to cleanse the land of blood shed upon it. We understand we are not asking forgiveness for the person, but only on behalf of the sin committed by them, against the Lord. Lord, we are the people that You are searching for to make up the hedge on behalf of this land.

> *And I sought for a man among them that should make up the hedge, and stand in the gap before me for the land, that I should not destroy it: but I found none.* —Ezekiel 22:30

Pour your juice into each cup, waiting to drink of it until the proper time. There are several ways to do this; each person can have a small cup of juice or wine, or there can be one cup that is passed around. After the prayer, the remainder of the juice will be poured on the land and over the bread.

The leader reads the scriptures and decrees and prays:

> *For this is my blood of the New Testament, which is shed for many for the remission of sins.* —Matthew 26:28

> *After the same manner also he took the cup, when he had supped, saying, this cup is the New Testament in my blood: this do ye, as oft as ye drink it, in remembrance of me.* —I Corinthians 11:25

Lord, we raise this cup to You as a memorial of remembrance for Your blood that You shed on the cross to redeem us and our land from sin. We read in scriptures that You asked the Father to forgive those who were guilty of Your death (Luke 23:34). Then You died, and a soldier pierced Your side and blood and water flowed out onto the ground (John 19:30-34).

We are reminded of that shedding of Your blood upon the ground, along with Your prayer for forgiveness.

The debt of sin has been paid in full through the shed blood of Jesus. We have been redeemed from death to life. We are symbolically applying blood for blood on the land, as we have repented for the sin committed against You on this land or in this region, including the shedding of innocent blood through abortions. We thank You for restoring this land from death to life. Amen.

Drink about half of the cup; then pour the remainder on top of the bread that is on the ground.

The leader reads:

As we take of the drink offering and pour the remainder into the mouth of the land, may it drink deeply, to the very foundation of its beginnings, and be cleansed from all spiritual liens.

This is a witness to Heaven and Earth of the renewing and restoration of covenant. We ask that the land would return to You, Lord. It will shout jubilee—freedom from bondage!

We bind this land to the purposes and destiny that the Lord intended for it. Amen.

Step 4. Pouring of the Oil

Pour half of the anointing oil over the bread and wine, as a symbol of the Holy Spirit and His Light. The remainder of the oil will be poured on the top of the memorial stone.

The leader decrees:

As agents of light, we pour this oil onto the land as an emblem of the Lord's anointing and the light of the Holy Spirit. We bind the light of the Lord to the land. It shall flood down to the very foundation, illuminating and driving out all darkness. Darkness will flee in terror from this property, never to rob our harvest again, as the supernatural presence of the Lord establishes a permanent position on this land.

As we pour the healing oil of Your consolation into the wounds of our land, it shall bring forth Shalom peace, prosperity, wellness, happiness, friendliness, welfare, health, favor, rest, safety and overall wellbeing of the Lord. It shall be a place from which shall flow ministry to all nations and peoples of the world, and blessings and honor to our Lord and Savior. May it be a continual river of praise and worship unto our God and His Christ.

Financial blessing and generational wealth will spring forth from its depths, with wisdom and honor as its resting place. No evil shall come near any one who treads upon this land and who seeks its rest.

> *Light is sown for the righteous, and gladness for the upright in heart. —Psalm 97:11*

Step 5.   Plant a symbol of abundant provision

Corn, wine, and oil are mentioned together eighteen times in the Bible. They represent the fruitfulness of the ground, God's good gifts; they are representative of the fertility of the country.

Many times the Lord refers to seeds as representatives of lives. As seeds are planted in the physical, we will reap in both the spiritual and physical realm. These seeds represent a prophetic harvest coming upon the earth. The way the earth gets harvested is through His people, who are His hands on the earth. The Lord will use you to plant seeds of the living God.

Place your symbol, or symbols, of abundant provision for the future generations into the ground and quote these scriptures;

> *Then shall he give the rain of thy seed that thou shalt sow the ground withal; and bread of the increase of the earth, and it shall be fat and plenteous: in that day shall thy cattle feed in large pastures. —Isaiah 30:23*

> *Therefore God give thee of the dew of heaven, and the fatness of the earth, and plenty of corn and wine: --Genesis 27:28*
> *The Lord will indeed give what is good, and our land will yield its harvest. —Psalm 85:12 (NIV)*

> *He that goeth forth and weepeth, bearing precious seed, shall doubtless come again with rejoicing, bringing his sheaves with him. —Psalm 126:6*

For the seed shall be prosperous; the vine shall give her fruit, and the ground shall give her increase, and the heavens shall give their dew; and I will cause the remnant of this people to possess all these things. —Zechariah 8:12

Step 6. Milk and honey -- a symbol of provision and sweetness of the land

You can pour milk and honey onto the land.

The leader decrees:

If the LORD delight in us, then he will bring us into this land, and give it us; a land which floweth with milk and honey. —Numbers 14:8

How sweet are thy words unto my taste! yea, sweeter than honey to my mouth! —Psalm 119:103

This land shall be a place of refreshing and supply. In this place the work of our hands shall be blessed with the good fruit of our labor. Investments of time and capital shall be multiplied by the favor of the Lord.

Prayers and petitions of unity and faith to the Lord shall pass through an open heaven to settle on His ears and cause His hands to move with favor and speed. Health and healing shall dwell here and go forth from here as a blessing to all that it encounters. Friends and family shall dwell here and be fruitful here. This land shall flow with milk and honey. Amen.

Step 7. Pour water on the land as a symbol of cleansing

A literal pouring out of water, oil or wine has long been symbolic of a person's pouring out all of himself, with no reservation, even his blood, in devotion to his Maker.

Then Samuel said, "Assemble all Israel at Mizpah, and I will intercede with the LORD for you." When they had assembled at Mizpah, they drew water and poured it out before the LORD. On that day they fasted and there they confessed, "We have sinned against the LORD." —1 Samuel 7:5-7 (NIV)

"There are three that bear witness in earth, the Spirit and the water, and the blood: and these three agree." —1 John 5:8

...pour out your heart like water before the presence of the Lord. —Lamentations 2:19 (NIV)

The water cleanses and delivers. We are sanctifying and purifying the land. Water is a symbol of baptism unto repentance, which delivers from the old, into regeneration and new life. God has delivered the human race many times through water: Noah and the flood, Moses as a baby, Moses and the Hebrew children through the Red Sea, Jonah, who was delivered out of the deep waters to bring salvation to Nineveh, and babies are delivered through the breaking of the waters.

The leader decrees:

Lord, as we pour this water our hearts are full of repentance, yet filled with faith; we are poured out before You. This water being poured is a memorial of remembrance to You, Lord, for all of the times You have delivered Your people through the water into new life. Fill us, Lord, with a renewal of Your Spirit in us. Create new hearts within us. Flood our ground with new life. Amen.

Step 8.   Bury evidence of the testimony of the new "Spiritual" Title Deed

Take the new, completed Title Deed and place it in a container of some sort to preserve it. This deed shows the land has a clear title and that it belongs to the Lord.

The following scripture notes that a container was necessary to preserve the title. The Israelites were taken away from this land, so when they returned the title would be proof of ownership of the property. The 'earthen vessels' are also known as Qumran Jars, and are available on our website for those who want to use them.

Thus saith the LORD of hosts, the God of Israel; Take these evidences, this evidence of the purchase, both which is sealed, and this evidence which is open; and put them in an earthen vessel, that they may continue many days. —Jeremiah 32:14

The leader decrees:

> Father we bless Your name this day. Thank You for giving our land a new prophetic name so it can smoothly transition into its destiny with new life. This land is now called _____.

Step 9. Build an altar or memorial

Bury your container with the Title Deed and any other items you are including. Place a stone or stones on top as an altar to the Lord. This is a symbol of a memorial to the goodness and greatness of our God.

The leader decrees:

> This land is married to the Lord, ordained unto holiness.

> *For you will have a covenant with the stones of the field, and the wild animals will be at peace with you. —Job 5:23 (NIV)*

> This stone is a witness.

> *And Joshua said unto all the people, Behold, this stone shall be a witness unto us; for it hath heard all the words of the LORD which he spake unto us: it shall be therefore a witness unto you, lest ye deny your God. —Joshua 24:27*

> *And David built there an altar to the Lord, and offered burnt offerings and peace offerings. So the Lord heeded the prayers for the land and the plague was withdrawn from Israel. —2 Samuel 24:25*

> *Then will I remember my covenant with Jacob, and also my covenant with Isaac, and also my covenant with Abraham will I remember; and I will remember the land. —Leviticus 26:42*

Pour some oil upon the altar of the Lord.

> *Then Jacob took the stone that had been under his head, and set it up as a memorial of the place where God had appeared to him. He poured oil on top of it. He called the name of that place Bethel The House of God. Then he made a vow and consecrated the land.   —Genesis 28: 18-19 (NKJV)*

You can add other items around the altar of memorial, as you are led.

Step 10. Decree blessing over the land

Now that we have completed the nine previous steps, which could symbolize 9 months of pregnancy, we have birthed the baby we could call Restoration, and now we are ready to move into the new birth of our lives and our land.

> *Listen to these ordinances, be true to them and observe them and in return Yahweh, your God, will be true to the covenant. He will bless the produce of your soil, your corn, your wine, and your oil. —Deuteronomy 7 12-13 (author's paraphrase)*
>
> *Surely his salvation is near to those who honor him; our land will be filled with his glory. —Psalm 85:9 (NIV)*
>
> *And the LORD shall make thee plenteous in goods, in the fruit of thy body, and in the fruit of thy cattle, and in the fruit of thy ground, in the land which the LORD swore unto thy fathers to give thee. The LORD shall open unto thee his good treasure, the heaven to give the rain unto thy land in his season, and to bless all the work of thine hand: and thou shalt lend unto many nations, and thou shalt not borrow.*
> *—Deuteronomy 28:11-12*

Prayer of Blessing over the land

The leader decrees:

This land shall be a place of courage and spiritual encounter; of salvation and new beginnings; of faith and hope. From this place shall go the generations of this family to the utter most parts of the world to establish the Kingdom of God, to bless His Holy Name, and to be a blessing to every people group and every nation of the earth.

All manner of creative ideas shall flow into the inhabitants of this land from the mind of God including (but not limited to) visual and performing arts, inventions, solutions to world problems and an overall willingness to serve God and His people. Financial rewards and righteous living shall spring forth to all the generations initiated on this land and all who are related to them by blood or covenant. Blessed shall they be as they come in and blessed shall they be as they go out, throughout the generations and the eternity in which they exist. Godly humility is their brand and Godly favor is their portion. Amen

Finish by quoting Psalm 91 as a covering protection

The enemy will be able to see the effects or results of our prayers, but he won't be able to see where the prayers are coming from when we quote these verses at the beginning or conclusion of any intercession, because we will be hidden under the wings of the Lord as we pray.

He that dwelleth in the secret place of the most High shall abide under the shadow of the Almighty. I will say of the LORD, He is my refuge and my fortress: my God; in him will I trust. Surely he shall deliver thee from the snare of the fowler, and from the noisome pestilence.

He shall cover thee with His feathers, and under his wings shalt thou trust: his truth shall be thy shield and buckler. Thou shalt not be afraid for the terror by night; nor for the arrow that flieth by day; Nor for the pestilence that walketh in darkness; nor for the destruction that wasteth at noonday. A thousand shall fall at thy side, and ten thousand at thy right hand; but it shall not come nigh thee.

Only with thine eyes shalt thou behold and see the reward of the wicked. Because thou hast made the LORD, which is my refuge, even the most High, thy habitation; there shall no evil befall thee, neither shall any plague come nigh thy dwelling.

For he shall give his angels charge over thee, to keep thee in all thy ways. They shall bear thee up in their hands, lest thou dash thy foot against a stone. Thou shalt tread upon the lion and adder: the young lion and the dragon shalt thou trample under feet.

Because he hath set his love upon me, therefore will I deliver him: I will set him on high, because he hath known my name. He shall call upon me, and I will answer him: I will be with him in trouble; I will deliver him, and honor him. With long life will I satisfy him, and shew him my salvation. Amen.
—Psalm 91:1-16

Other enactments

Let worship and justice kiss! Sing some songs to the Lord. Play a CD of praise and worship, and sing along. Wave flags, tabrets, and streamers. Blow a shofar or two. Dance and rejoice.

You can place a banner over the altar like Moses did

Banners are displayed to claim rulership, or possession of a piece of land. *Nissi* in Hebrew means banner. Jesus is our Banner.

> *And Moses built an altar, and called the name of it Jehovah-Nissi.* —Exodus 17:15

Be bold in your faith! Here is your opportunity to do a great exploit for the Lord and for your land!

For those reading this book who have never done anything like this, the Bible directs us to move in faith, believing the Word of God. He will meet us where we are. The Word says faith without works is dead.

> *By faith Noah, when warned about things not yet seen, in holy fear built an ark to save his family. By his faith he condemned the world and became heir of the righteousness that comes by faith. By faith Abraham, when called to go to a place he would later receive as his inheritance, obeyed and went, even though he did not know where he was going.* —Hebrews 11:7-8

Step out in faith and receive the blessings of the Lord!

Title Deed

To all parties with any interest in the land formally known as (address)

_____

It will be known as _____

This land is now, and shall remain free from any ungodly spiritual encumbrances or liens of the kind from this day through eternity, because of the saving grace of the shed blood of Jesus Christ.

This land is hereby freely transferred to Jehovah God with a clear title.

Witness _____

Date _____

Witness _____

Date _____

PAID IN FULL BY THE BLOOD

From God's Hands to your land

About the author

 Jeanette is in active ministry. In 1997, she and her husband, Bud, founded and are the co-owners of Glorious Creations. Glorious Creations is a Worship and Praise adornment company. Jeanette is ordained as a minister through Gospel Crusade and has been in full time ministry since 1998. She has written two other books, *Heavenly Impact: Symbolic Praise, Worship and Intercession* and *From the Courtroom of Judgment to the Throne Room of Grace and Mercy.*

She is an officer in Aglow International and is an Intercessor Co-coordinator for Southwest Michigan under the leadership of Apostle Barbara Yoder, Leader of the Breakthrough Apostolic Ministries Network, and Apostle Doug Carr, Regional Director for the Network.

Bless Your Land Kit

This Kit makes a perfect gift!

It contains: 1 Book, 4 communion cups with wafers, Milk and Honey, Harvest Seeds, Consecration Oil, A Title Deed. (Just add water)

Other resources from Jeanette Strauss

Heavenly Impact

Symbolic Praise, Worship, and Intercession.

"On Earth As It Is In Heaven"

This book is a must read for those seeking a Biblical foundation for the use of symbolic tools of praise, worship and intercession. This information presents clear guidelines concerning their proper place and use.

Explore the Possibilities!

Heavenly Impact guides you through history and explains the relevance of worship adornment as it identifies strategic value. Scripture references reveal that our actions on earth truly do have a "Heavenly Impact". Tools covered: Flags, Billows, Mat-teh', Shofar, Streamers, Tabrets, and Veils, vocabulary of movement, and Biblical color symbolism.

A 12 week course, the *Teachers Manual and Student Workbook* is now available for the book *Heavenly Impact*. This is an easy to understand and teach course. At the end of each chapter are Prophetic exercises and activations, discussion topics, and a biblical color chart. Purchase as a set with the *Heavenly Impact* book, or individually.

From the Courtroom of Heaven
to the Throne Room of Grace and Mercy

As a born-again Christian, I had never given the Courtroom of Heaven a thought. Then, in answer to our prayer for our backslidden daughter, the Lord gave me a dream. The dream contained the proper protocol to use in the Courtroom of Heaven on her behalf. As a result, she was set free and restored.

This book includes the dream and the strategy the Lord revealed. You can use this same protocol and win your own petitions in the Courtroom of Heaven. Show up where the accuser of the brethren does not expect, and win your case!

Glorious Creations

1114 Robinson Road, Quincy, Michigan 49082
517-639-4395 www.gloriouscreations.net

ORDER FORM

	Price	Quantity	Total

From God's Hand to Your Land
   $10.00 each   x _____ = _____

De las Manos de Dios a Tu Tierra
   $10.00 each   x _____ = _____

Land Kit $20.00 each   x _____ = _____

Title Deed $1.00 each   x _____ = _____

Courtroom of Heaven
   $14.00 each   x _____ = _____

Prayers and Petitions
   $13.00 each   x _____ = _____

Heavenly Impact
   $14.00 each   x _____ = _____

Heavenly Impact Teachers Manual
   $ 15.00 each   x _____ = _____

Heavenly Impact Student Workbook
   $13.00 each   x _____ = _____

Total Due for Product   _____

Shipping & Handling   _____

Total Amount Due   _____

Shipping & Handling:

0 - $9.99	$ 4.00
$10 - $19.99	$ 6.00
$20.00 - $39.99	$ 8.00
$40.00 - $60.00	$10.00

We ship Priority Mail

Oct 7. 2016

This
Belongs

TO:
Samantha
Michel